A LITTLE MOOSE and WOLFIE Book

MINDFULNESS for VIKINGS

Leo Hartas
&
Amanda Boulter

D1059476

FAERHAVEN PRESS

To
freya
fin
Isaac
Inigo
felix

With special thanks to Camille
www.howtolivewell.co.uk

A LITTLE MOOSE and WOLFIE Book

MINDFULNESS for VIKINGS

Leo Hartas
&
Amanda Boulter

A Faerhaven Press Book
www.faerhavenpress.com

find more Little Moose books and stories at
www.littlemoosestory.com

Copyright©2017
Leo Hartas & Amanda Boulter

ISBN: 978=1=9999011=0=3

All rights reserved. No part of this book may be reproduced, stored in a retrieval system, or transmitted, in any form or by any means, electronic or mechanical, by photocopying, recording or otherwise, without prior permission in writing from the publisher.

Concept and text by Leo & Amanda
Illustration by Leo

Design in Serif PagePlus by Leo & Amanda
Font, Little Moose, created by Leo

"I believe that the very purpose of life is to be happy."
Dalai Lama XIV

Being a Viking
can be tough.

All the axe
wielding and
battling
play havoc with
inner peace.

That's when
mindfulness
can really help.

Just one deep breath
makes a difference,
helping us step
calmly on our way.

Little Moose and Wolfie
live in the moment,
just being themselves,
feeling the joy of nature
and the playfulness of life.

They call it moosing around.

We call it

Mindfulness
for Vikings.

Just this

Moosing around

feet on the ground
head in the clouds

Even the little moments
are big moments

It's not work if it feels like play

Say yes to the mess

It takes guts to do
the boring things

Just rest

The world is full of magic

It's all so big and beautiful

No battle was ever won in bed

Oh well

Today is do nothing day

Going with the flow

Sometimes you have to let go

feel the buzz

There's being alive ... and there's

being alive!

finding balance

The grumbling is the hardest part

My home is on the earth

To grow a forest you only have to
plant the first seed

Share the love

Always pick the easy one first

Deep breath!

All is well

Wherever I am
I'm right here

Howling with the wolves

No burden is too great
for a friend

Slow and sure is the way

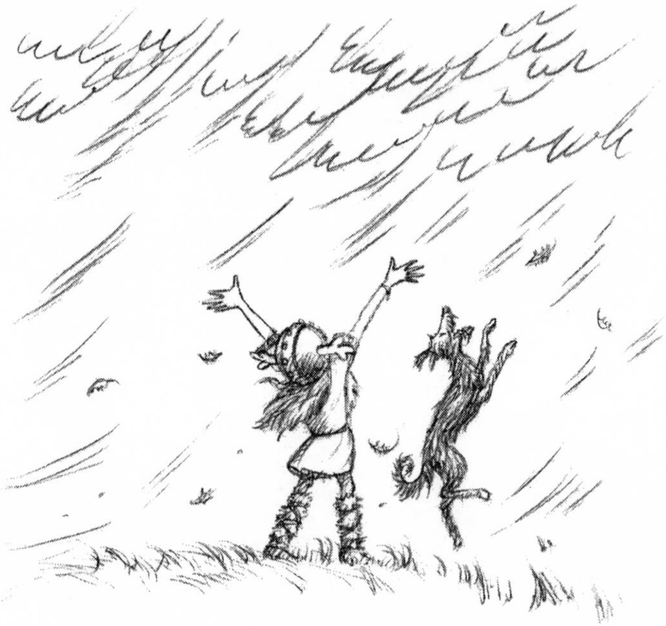

I am the storm!

Laugh at life's little surprises

Today I will relish every step

Wet feet can be fun

Who dares wins

Create your masterpiece

Leap into Life

Keep trying
and you'll find your spark

Everybody loves somebody

Don't let small fears stop big
adventures

A glimpse into
the world of
Little Moose
and Wolfie

Through the Dragon's Throat
Across the Darkwater
Beneath the Wall
At the Edge of the World
Lies the village of Faerhaven

And there

Under the watchful eye of Odin
Lives a boy called Little Moose
(and his dog Wolfie)

Little Moose

Wolfie

Odin knows their future
He knows the adventures ahead
He knows that they will be heroes

   Long remembered
      in tales sung and said

faerhaven

FAERHAVEN
Over the Darkwater

DARKWATER

← The Dragon's Throat

FYLKEFJORD

Follow the adventures of
Little Moose from a baby
to a young adult

Look out for these new series
beginning 2018

Playful tales for toddlers.

Exciting stories in picture books and chapter books for early and confident readers.

Challenging adventures for teens and young adults.

COMING SOON
December 2017

A DOG'S GUIDE to DRAGONS

Despite their hard won reputation for being a bit daft, it's a little known fact that dogs are very knowledgeable about dragons.

Join Wolfie and his human Little Moose for a dog's guide to these fascinating creatures.

A book of sage advice and delightful illustrations to help you discover the dragons in your own life.

For a free dragon gift and news of when A Dog's Guide to Dragons is out sign up for our newsletter at

www.littlemoosestory.com

A LITTLE MOOSE and WOLFIE BOOK

A DOG'S GUIDE to DRAGONS

Leo Hartas & Amanda Boulter

FAERHAVEN PRESS

Read on for a little taster ...

Dragons are everywhere.

Most humans don't believe that.
But it's true.

Wolfie knows all
about dragons.

Little Moose
knows a little
too, but not as
much as Wolfie.

Even the best
humans don't
always see
what's in front
of them.

Wolfie says there are five kinds of dragons.

Tree dragons are the littlest.
Water dragons are the middlest.
And rock dragons are the biggest.

Fire dragons come in every size
and are always swooping about.
That's why even humans can see fire dragons.

Spirit dragons come in all sizes too.
They can be as big as a
mountain or as small
as a bird.

But humans can only
glimpse spirit dragons
from the corner
of their eye.

Ssh! Keep still

Moosing around

Sign up to our newsletter
and get your free
Christmas Dragon
to download, print and make.
www.littlemoosestory.com

Leo Hartas has been illustrating children's books, magazines, comics and games for over 30 years. He finds his own inner calm running around a field in Devon, England dressed as Viking. He lives in a tumbledown cottage and has a white fluffy cat called Dracula.

Amanda Boulter has spent many hours sitting on a cushion doing nothing (meditating). She has a black and white dog called Jess who likes chewing the piano (but it still works). She teaches creative writing at the University of Winchester, England.

We'd love to hear from you
Please leave us a review

80536718R00064

Made in the USA
Lexington, KY
03 February 2018